10½ Things
No Commencement Speaker
Has Ever Said

Also by Charles Wheelan

Naked Economics:
Undressing the Dismal Science

10½ Things
No Commencement Speaker
Has Ever Said

Charles Wheelan

Illustrations by Peter Steiner

W. W. NORTON & COMPANY

NEW YORK · LONDON

For information about permission to reproduce selections from this book,
write to Permissions, W. W. Norton & Company, Inc.,
500 Fifth Avenue, New York, NY 10110

For information about special discounts for bulk purchases, please contact
W. W. Norton Special Sales at specialsales@wwnorton.com or 800-233-4830

Manufacturing by Courier Westford
Book design by Joe Lops
Production manager: Devon Zahn

Library of Congress Cataloging-in-Publication Data

Wheelan, Charles J.
10 1/2 things no commencement speaker has ever said / Charles Wheelan ;
illustrations by Peter Steiner. — 1st ed.
    p. cm.
Includes bibliographical references (p.   ).
ISBN 978-0-393-07431-4 (hardcover)
1. Conduct of life. I. Title. II. Title: Ten and a half things
no commencement speaker has ever said.
BJ1589.W44 2012
170'.44—dc23
                                    2012005123

W. W. Norton & Company, Inc., 500 Fifth Avenue, New York, N.Y. 10110
www.wwnorton.com

W. W. Norton & Company Ltd., Castle House, 75/76 Wells Street, London W1T 3QT

1 2 3 4 5 6 7 8 9 0

For the Dartmouth Class of 2011

Contents

Introduction

This book is adapted from a speech I gave during Commencement weekend at Dartmouth College in June of 2011. I was not the commencement speaker. That was Conan O'Brien. (As my friends have since been all too happy to point out, I was just the warm-up act.) Instead, I spoke the day before commencement, on Class Day, which may be an exercise unique to Dartmouth. The purpose of Class Day is to bring the graduating class together for one final meeting. There are some parents and guests, but mostly it is just the graduating students. The event is completely informal. When the weather is good, Class Day is held outdoors in a clearing in the middle of a pine forest. The students, wearing the usual casual college attire, sit on the ground. When the weather is bad, the event is held in the campus field house, but the students still sit on the ground, so that the effect is oddly intimate for a gathering of a thousand people in a space designed for indoor track meets.

Whereas commencement is about public pomp and circumstance, Class Day is more about quiet reflection. It is a day for and about the students in the graduating class. There are only three significant speeches: one given by the class president, one by a student chosen by the class, and one by a faculty member, also chosen by the class.

I was the faculty speaker. This was somewhat unusual in that I was not actually on the Dartmouth faculty at the time. I was teaching at the University of Chicago. However, I had visited Dartmouth for many years to teach during the summer term that is required for all students at the end of their second year—the so-called sophomore summer. Many of the graduating seniors had been my students. Still, I suspect that if there was some kind of *Bush v. Gore* challenge before the Supreme Court as to my eligibility to be the faculty speaker, I most likely would have lost.

More important, this was a tremendous honor and a meaningful day, even if I was just the warm-up act for Conan O'Brien (who by all accounts gave a very nice speech the next day). I am a Dartmouth graduate. Twenty-three years earlier, I had attended my own Class Day, outdoors on a nearly perfect spring morning. I remember each one of the speakers (if not necessarily what they said). I sat on the ground that day with my classmate and girlfriend—to whom I have now been married for nineteen years, or nearly as long as most of the students in the Class of 2011 have been alive. For the record, when I told the Dartmouth '11s that I have been married to my Dartmouth girlfriend for nearly two decades, it was one of the biggest applause lines of the day, which says something about either a yearning among young people for old-fashioned values or a shortage of applause lines elsewhere in the speech.

In short, the 2011 Class Day was a moment of great significance for the students, and also for me as a professor and returning alumnus.

But what to say?

There was no way I could give a saccharine, conventional graduation-type speech. I had become sick of commencement speeches not long after my own graduation. My first real job out of college was writing speeches for the governor of Maine. Every spring, I would draft extraordinary tidbits of wisdom for twenty-two-year-olds—even though I was only twenty-four myself when I first started offering that wisdom. The Dartmouth speech demanded more than my old clichés and nonoffensive jokes (which were also, much to my chagrin, non-funny).

I knew there were plenty of things that students would be interested in hearing, since I had literally been sitting where they would be sitting. Yes, commencement is a time of excitement and promise, but I also remember it as a time of anxiety and self-doubt. In hindsight, there were things that I wish someone had told me. Eventually that line of thinking gave me the insight I needed to write the speech. I would tell the Class of 2011 what I wished someone had told the Class of 1988, particularly the nonconventional advice that would have prepared me—and that I hoped would prepare them—for some of the rough patches that lay ahead.

From that idea, the speech was born: "Five Things No Commencement Speaker Has Ever Said." However, due to a numbering error, there were actually "six things." The speech I delivered at Dartmouth had two number 4s. (Perfection is overrated.) Each one of those points, including both number 4s, was something I would have liked to hear on my Class Day. In a surprising way, many of the points I wanted to make intersected with my work as a faculty member. I teach economics and public policy. One of my passionate interests as an academic is the study of happiness and well-being, about which we now know a great deal. Could I weave together the insights I wish someone had offered me on that beautiful sunny day in 1988 with some of the more intriguing things I have learned since about leading "the good life"?

As I noted, Class Day is informal, except for one nod to tradition: the graduating students are led by a bagpiper through the streets on campus and into the field house. Imagine the plaintive yet lovely wail of bagpipes as the senior class assembled together for one last time before their graduation, to hear from a professor and faculty member who had engaged in the very same exercise twenty-three years earlier.

What follows is what I said, more or less.

10½ Things
No Commencement Speaker
Has Ever Said

Your time in fraternity basements was well spent.

Seriously, you can Google that. No Commencement speaker has ever said it. Go back to the Greeks, the Romans. Never. But I am serious. Obviously my point is broader than just fraternity basements. I am referring to the time you spent playing intramural sports, working on the school newspaper, or just lounging outside with friends on a perfect fall day. There was work you could have been doing instead—and there always will be. That is the point.

Researchers are now studying happiness. They are literally asking, "What makes us enjoy life?" What we now know—what comes up as significant in every study of well-being using every possible methodology—is that one of the most important causal factors associated with happiness and well-being is your meaningful connections with other human beings: family, friends, organizations, neighbors, social movements. In other words, the people around you at commencement.

One of our most intriguing sources of data is the Harvard Study of Adult Development. Beginning in 1937, this study followed Harvard sophomores for seventy years: through graduation, marriages, careers, and illness, and, in some cases, death. The value of this kind of longitudinal study is that you can follow the same people over decades and make meaningful inferences about what behaviors in life are associated with what outcomes, in terms of health, career success, coping with adversity, and an overall sense of well-being.

The participants in the Harvard study were mostly white men, which reflected the times. In other respects, particularly their education and promise, they looked very much like a contemporary college cohort. The results of the study are fascinating. I will draw your attention to just one. When the director of the study was asked what he had learned from decades of data on Harvard students, he replied, "That the only thing that really matters in life are your relationships to other people."

The Harvard study is not an anomaly. The same pattern keeps popping up. *New York Times* columnist David Brooks wrote recently about a study which found that joining a group that meets just once a month has the same effect on your sense of well-being as *doubling your income*. He writes, "The overall impression from this research is that economic and professional success exists on the surface of life, and that they emerge out of interpersonal relationships, which are much deeper and more important."

Now, having urged you to spend guilt-free time in fraternity basements, I feel compelled to point out that alcohol abuse is the most common way that otherwise privileged people fall on seriously hard times. By the time the men in the Harvard study had reached retirement, one of the most significant factors associated with healthy aging, both physically and psychologically, was not abusing alcohol. (The others were education, a stable marriage, not smoking, getting some exercise, maintaining a healthy weight, and employing "mature adaptations," which are constructive reactions to life's inevitable setbacks.)

So, bear in mind that I am promoting fraternity basements because of the camaraderie, not necessarily the libations. In that vein, look around at your classmates. Certainly one benchmark of your post-graduation success could be how many of your peers are still your close friends in ten or twenty years. You will also develop other meaningful life relationships that provide the same kind of camaraderie. The research tells us that if you get that right, most everything else will fall into place.

P. Steiner

Some of your worst days lie ahead.

Commencement speakers usually steer clear of this theme. I know that graduation is a happy event. I know that you are all rich with promise. I know that you will someday run companies, and maybe even the country. Clearly, one fun part of being out of college for twenty years is looking around at my classmates who are doing fabulously cool things. But I promised you unconventional advice. So I am here to tell you that between today and twenty years from now, and even then at some points, there are going to be some stretches that are just plain awful. And trust me, as a writer, I do not choose those words lightly. If you are going to do anything worthwhile—write, invent, start a company, lead a social movement—you will face extended periods of grinding self-doubt and failure. And when you get to these tough moments, *because you will get there*, I want you to remember two stories.

The first is about my roommate from senior year, who remains a great friend. John really wanted to be an investment banker. All senior winter he attended every corporate information session, always wearing a suit. He sat in the front row. He read books on interviewing strategies. Those of us who knew him well didn't think he was particularly suited for Wall Street, but that is where he aimed to go.

He did not get a job during corporate recruiting. He did not get a job during senior spring, when even the people who had been unsuccessful during corporate recruiting got jobs at less prestigious and relatively unknown firms, like Microsoft. He did not get a job during the summer. He did not get a job in the fall. (Yes, I realize this sounds like a job search handbook written by Dr. Seuss.) John moved in with his mother in San Francisco and began studying Japanese, since we were all convinced that Japan was taking over the world. (The Japanese real estate, stock market, and banking collapses were roughly one year away.)

I visited John in October after graduation, when he still had had no offers from Wall Street firms and no opportunities in investment banking in San Francisco. In fact, he had had only one job offer: assistant food and beverage manager at a hotel on the island of Saipan. Just by way of background, Saipan is twelve miles long, five miles wide, and in the middle of the Pacific Ocean. When people want to have a good time on Saipan, they fly to Guam.

John was, and still is, one of the most polite and urbane people I know. So other than being a single guy on a small rock in the middle of the Pacific Ocean, the hospitality industry actually made a lot of sense. I told him to go. Remember, it was October after graduation and he was living with his mother.

On that little island, John met his future wife, a woman from New Zealand who also happened to find work in Saipan. And he never left the hospitality industry. He went on to become CEO of Rosewood Hotels.

The second story is my own. My bout of crushing self-doubt came almost exactly one year after I had urged John to take the job in Saipan. The reason I was staying with John in San Francisco during that October after graduation was that I was embarking on a trip around the world. From San Francisco, I would head to Los Angeles, then Tahiti, New Zealand, and beyond. This trip was one of the most important and formative undertakings in my life. You will hear more about that later. For now, let's fast-forward to my *return* from traveling around the world, roughly nine months later.

I came back with a lot of great pictures, some awesome stories, and a refined sense of what I wanted to do in life—but no job and no money. When I say "no money," I mean that my net worth consisted of less than a thousand dollars, including my bicycle and golf clubs. Most of my friends, even John, had been working for the better part of a year. I had no idea what I would do next, other than a vague inclination that I wanted to be a writer.

I went back to Dartmouth to use the career services office. I wrote articles for the alumni magazine to keep myself busy and to earn a little money. I had sublet an apartment on campus from some students who were gone for the summer. Every day I scoured job listings and sent out resumés. The world was not clamoring to hire me.

And then one day, the students from whom I had sublet the apartment came back—with no advance notice, I might add. I went down to Boston for the weekend, but I knew that when I returned to Hanover, I had literally no place to go. My pathetic existence had been downgraded to no job, no money, *and* no place to live. My classmates were long gone, so I called the one person I knew well in Hanover, Bill Scherman, or as I called him until the day he died, Mr. Scherman.

Mr. Scherman was a member of the Class of 1934, making him roughly fifty years older than I was. He had retired with his wife to Hanover and had been kind enough to help me and several other students with a newspaper that we had founded. I figured that if I could stay with Mr. Scherman and his wife when I returned to town on that Sunday night, then I could find a new place to live on Monday.

I made the call to the Schermans from Boston. I explained my circumstances. I remember asking nervously, "Mr. Scherman, I was hoping that I might be able to stay at your house tonight."

I lived with Mr. and Mrs. Scherman for three months. I would spend the days doing freelance writing and looking for a job. In the evening, Mrs. Scherman would cook dinner for the three of us and then we would watch the news together. In hindsight, of course, I recognize that this was a profound act of kindness and generosity on their part. At the time, as I sat on the couch every evening watching television with a seventy-year-old couple, I was thinking, "My life cannot get any worse."

Oh, but it did. I continued to interview unsuccessfully for jobs. Many firms rejected me. I, too, rejected some of them. I still had visions of writing for a living, or of at least doing something that I would find interesting and intellectually engaging. On occasion, I would finish a day of interviews, and some manager at the firm would ask, "Well, what do you think?"

I would say something along the lines of, "I don't think it's a great fit for me."

When my parents found out about this, they nearly had a collective stroke, if that's physically possible. *College graduates who haven't worked in a year and have $274 in liquid assets and are living in the guest bedroom of a seventy-year-old couple do not turn down jobs!*

They had a point. Even now, I will concede that. I promised my mother that I would greet any future job opportunity with great eagerness, no matter what the underlying reality might be.

Soon I had my test case. I interviewed for a job as a "technical writer," admittedly without much understanding of what a technical writer actually does. Suffice it to say that this is not how Hemingway got his start. Have you ever read the instructions telling you how to replace the bag on your vacuum cleaner? That is what a technical writer pens. I spent an hour interviewing with a guy who was working on his opus: a human resources manual for a Fortune 500 company.* Everything about this job seemed miserable, including many of the people doing it.

---

* For the sake of disclosure, let me be clear: I would advise any aspiring writer to write anything that anyone will pay you to write. At various times in life, I have been paid to write all of the following: 1) an instruction book for a portable phone that could also work as a remote control for your television; 2) a guide for Sony retailers explaining why consumers should buy a regular television even though HD televisions would soon be released; 3) moving tips for a U.S. Post Office change-of-address kit; and 4) a series of job search guides sponsored by Honda Motors.

When the day of interviews drew to a close, I reached my moment of truth. Would I honor the promise to my mother? Or would I tell the employer candidly that this firm seemed like a tar pit where all of my dreams and ambitions would die a slow, agonizing death?

One of the senior managers called me into his cubicle. "Well, what do you think about the job?" he asked.

These are the moments that define you in life. They are a portal into the soul. They illustrate starkly whether you will stay true to your ideals or buckle weakly in the face of parental and societal pressures.

I smiled as broadly as I possibly could and said, "I think this job would be terrific!"

They offered it to me. I had two weeks to let them know if I would take the position.

Fate intervened, as is so often the case. A few days later I stumbled across a posting for a job I knew I wanted immediately; the governor of Maine needed a new speechwriter. I interviewed for the job late in the week and started the following Monday—all within the two-week window that the technical writing folks had given me.

I was saved from the tar pit. More important, someone was going to pay me to write meaningful prose.

Don't make the world worse.

I know that I am supposed to tell you to aspire to greatness. But I am going to lower the bar here for a minute. I am going to ask first and foremost that you do not use your prodigious talents to mess the world up, because too many smart people are doing that already.

It's true that high school dropouts are more likely to steal cars or go to prison or end up on welfare. But if you really want to cause social mayhem, it helps to have a college degree. (And the Ivy Leaguers can be the worst of all.) To make that point, I want to speak for a moment about an iconic photograph from 1994 that embodies the capacity of smart, highly educated people to do really nasty things. In April of that year, the heads of seven major tobacco companies appeared before Congress. They were all sworn in. The famous photo I referred to is of the seven executives, all taking the oath at the same time.

All seven of them then proceeded to testify before Congress and the nation that cigarettes are not addictive. As I said, this was 1994—not 1924 or 1934. The Surgeon General had already reported that tobacco is as addictive as cocaine or heroin. In prepared testimony, William Campbell, president of Philip Morris, stated unequivocally, "Cigarette smoking is not addictive."

This is, by the way, after decades during which the same companies had deliberately obscured the causal relationship between smoking and cancer, despite plenty of research making that clear and compelling link.

The photo of the seven executives taking the oath is always etched in my mind. It sticks with me because time has wiped away any ambiguity about the real facts. We can see that scene for what it was: profound dishonesty, inspired by naked self-interest, and perpetrated by people who had plenty of other life options. In fact, I got to wondering recently, Where did those guys—and it was all men—go to school? Was it a community college? Had they not finished high school? Is that why they felt compelled to lie in a way that put millions of lives at risk? I asked my research assistant to look into it.

Among the seven who took the oath and testified that day that cigarettes are not addictive, there were a lot of impressive degrees. Three of them were from Harvard.

You are smart and motivated and creative. Everyone will tell you that you can change the world. They are right. I am going to remind you that "changing the world" also includes things like skirting financial regulations, obscuring climate-change research, designing sub-prime mortgages that low-income families won't understand, and selling unhealthy foods to increasingly obese children.

If you work hard and focus, you could probably be awesome at all of those dastardly deeds! Creative, even innovative—in a diabolically underhanded way. But, to paraphrase Nike, just don't do it.

I am not asking you to cure cancer here. I am just

asking you not to spread it—literally in the case of the unapologetically dishonest tobacco executives, but figuratively in the rest of your life.

If that is not enough, let me add parenthetically that this, too, will help make you happy. All of the research I have ever seen on this topic, including the aforementioned Harvard study, is very clear: leading a life with purpose, however you define that, is strongly associated with happiness and well-being.

Marry someone smarter than you are.

This is one of my most impressive accomplishments. I bring this point up for three reasons. First, for all of the controversy over marriage lately, there has been virtually no public discussion of the role that marriage plays in economic success. The students in my economics and public policy classes may remember my favorite quiz question of all time: "True or False: Dartmouth is the kind of place where assortive mating is going on."

This question is less sordid than it would appear. The answer is true; it merely refers to the fact that highly educated people tend to marry each other, as do poorly educated people. The result magnifies many of our underlying social trends, including income inequality.

To make this point much more personal, and because I have vowed to address things that no one told me when I was in college, I will tell you that what I have learned over time is that the benefits of marrying my Phi Beta Kappa classmate, whom I met at orientation freshman week, are not merely that she is fun and beautiful, but also that it's like having another economic oar in the water. When I was getting a PhD, she was working. When she wanted to start a software company, I had a steady income. When I wanted to take a year off to write books, she had a steady income. You are good at standardized tests; you get the pattern.

In addition to all of the advice that Dr. Phil can offer you about marriage, I am telling you that you are getting a professional teammate for life. So pick wisely.

Now the second reason I bring this subject up is that a healthy marriage will make you . . . yes, happy! We have got research on this too. In fact, the economists even think they can quantify it. In terms of happiness and well-being, a healthy marriage is the equivalent of earning an extra $100,000 a year. That said, I would urge you not to tell your future spouse that he or she will be worth roughly a million dollars at the end of ten years, since it never sounds as cool to everyone else as it does to the economists.

Finally, I bring up the benefit of smart partners because commencement is your chance! At many colleges, everyone who is a member of Phi Beta Kappa wears a pink-and-blue ribbon on their gown. Other institutions will print the names of the most distinguished graduates. Folks, this is the equivalent of hunting smart fish in a barrel. After graduation, you can't walk into a bar and ask for a list of the smartest 10 percent! At graduation, you can. Heck, you don't even have to ask—it's already printed in the program! Next year, when you go to the gym, the smartest and most hard-working individuals will not be wearing pink-and-blue ribbons. So pay attention while you have the chance.

Now, to those of you *wearing* the pink-and-blue ribbons: I am *not* telling you to continue wearing those ribbons after commencement. My wife sometimes wears hers around the house, and frankly, it's unseemly.

I'm sorry.

I assume that commencement speakers don't usually apologize. I am not aware that I have personally harmed any of you. But my generation has done a disservice to every young graduate, and so has the generation before mine. We have thrown a big, expensive party on your dime; you will have to clean up.

I'm forty-five years old, which is not much younger than the president of the United States. My generation is gradually replacing the "baby boomers" as the folks in charge. You are a graduate, so at least we have given you the benefit of an education to go along with your student loans. There has been no point in the history of human civilization when education will matter more. So, to paraphrase Bill

Murray in *Caddyshack*, "You've got that going for you."*

But in other respects, those of us in charge have totally abdicated our responsibilities to your generation and to those who will come after you. Tom Brokaw wrote a book about the World War II generation called *The Greatest Generation*. If he had written a book about our generation and those before us, it might have been called *The Marshmallow-Eating Generation*. I'll come back to what that title means in a moment, but for now, let's take a quick tour of what we have done for/to you.

We have lived egregiously beyond our means. You are literally and figuratively going to get our bills. If that sounds political, it's not meant to. It's just math and a little basic public finance. Leave aside whether government ought to spend more or less, and whether taxes ought to be higher or lower. Just look at the bottom line: the United States has accumulated $14 trillion in debt. If you think your student loans are bad, try

---

* If you have never seen *Caddyshack*, it's because you are from a different generation, which is relevant here.

this one out: the U.S. national debt—the $14 trillion we owe—is roughly $47,000 for each one of you.

As a policy wonk, I am tempted to add in the implicit obligations of the entitlement programs, such as Medicare and Social Security, which don't show up in the debt figures. They are expensive promises that we have made to ourselves. To be clear, I eventually expect to get these benefits, and you will pay for them—on top of your student loans and your $47,000 portion of the national debt.

You're welcome.

On the environmental front, our generation has refused to confront the challenge of climate change. As a policy person, the "controversy" over climate-change science reminds me a great deal of the decades in which tobacco executives obfuscated the relationship between smoking and cancer. At a minimum, the scientific uncertainty surrounding climate change has been a very convenient excuse for us to do nothing. Even the most intellectually dishonest person cannot construe "scientific uncertainty" to mean that we know with certainty that global warming is *not* happening. Thus, any reasonable person must concede that there is at least some risk of adverse climate change.

But let's step away from that largely fruitless scientific debate for a moment to think about climate change in the context of my generation and yours. In the United States, we have been unwilling to diminish our current standard of living in any significant way to protect against the risk of global warming. I will fully concede that that might turn out to be a defensible decision in the long run. But if not, what happens then? Who pays the price?

Not us. You do.

You're welcome for that too.

At this point, let me detour back to some crucial social science research. I claimed earlier that a Tom Brokaw book about our generation might be called *The Marshmallow-Eating Generation*. Here's why: In the late 1960s and early 1970s, researchers at Stanford University conducted a now-famous experiment using young children enrolled at Stanford's preschool facility. Experimenters sat the students at a table set with assorted objects that children of that age would find desirable (marshmallows, colored plastic poker chips, stick pretzels, and the like). The students were asked which of the objects they preferred.

Once that was determined, each student was offered an explicit choice that tested his or her ability to defer gratification: get a small reward now or a bigger reward later. The experimenter left the room, leaving a bell on the table in front of the student. If the student rang the bell before the experimenter returned, he or she would get a single marshmallow (or whatever other treat the student had chosen). However, if the student resisted ringing the bell until the experimenter returned (typically after fifteen or twenty minutes), he or she would hit the jackpot—at least in the eyes of a four-year-old. The reward was *two marshmallows*.

One remarkable finding from the study is that a student's ability at age four to defer gratification is correlated with better outcomes much later in life, such as academic and social success. For example, one follow-up paper found a significant positive association between how long students waited to ring the bell and—more than a decade later—their "ability to cope with frustration and stress in adolescence."

New York Times columnist David Brooks has cited this study and inferred that most social problems are rooted in an inability to defer gratification. He argues that for people with poor self-control, "life is a parade of foolish decisions: teen pregnancy, drugs, gambling, truancy and crime." I agree. I can find no other compelling explanation for why someone would do something as utterly ridiculous as dropping out of high school, no matter how bad the school is. (At crucial points in life you may want to remind yourself, If I can resist ringing the bell now, I will get more marshmallows later.)

In fact, I will see David Brooks and raise him one. I find myself asking an even bigger question: Is America as a nation losing its ability to wait for the second marshmallow? Can we still muster the political will and personal sacrifice to make investments today that will make us richer and stronger ten, twenty, or fifty years from now?

I asked myself this dispiriting question after re-reading a chapter on the history of American education that I had assigned to my public policy students. The chapter took the long view, describing two of America's most significant education policies *over the last several centuries*. First, states and communities (particularly in New England) offered broad access to taxpayer-supported public education from their earliest days. State laws in the eighteenth century required towns of a certain size to support a primary school. By the beginning of the nineteenth century, the United States had the highest literacy rate in the world.

Second, the young nation was remarkably aggressive in creating public universities. In 1862, President Lincoln signed the First Morrill Act, providing eleven million acres of public land to the states to enable them to set up what are now known as the land-grant universities—some of the preeminent research universities in the world to this day. Nearly every state joining the union after 1820 provided for a state university in its constitution. These are the places you might be graduating from.

Both of these developments (along with the later creation of high schools for the general public) help to explain America's remarkable economic performance in the nineteenth and twentieth centuries. As a nation, we systematically set aside a lot of marsh-mallows so that we would become more prosperous decades, even centuries later.

I am beginning to worry that Americans, both individually and in our collective decisions, are repeatedly opting for one marshmallow now instead of two later. As the huge national debt figures suggest, we are even gobbling up the marshmallows that rightfully belong to future generations. Instead of leaving more for those who come after us—things like world-class universities and interstate highways—we have left a note on the table explaining that any marshmallows available already belong to the Chinese (who, at present, have one of the highest savings rates in the world).

One of the follow-up studies using data from the Stanford marshmallow experiment states succinctly (and perhaps a little grandly for a study based on marshmallows, pretzels, and poker chips), "To be able to delay immediate satisfaction for the sake of future consequences has long been considered an essential achievement of human development."

Can we still do that?

My generation and the baby boomers ahead of us have set a horrible example. I am genuinely sorry about that, because it violates a long-standing pattern that has made this country strong, dynamic, and prosperous. I can only hope that you will do better.

Help stop the Little League arms race?

Several years ago, I ran for Congress. Suffice it to say that I did not finish first in the race (or second, or third, or fourth). On the morning after the primary, when most of us had been eliminated, the winner hosted a "unity breakfast" in which all of the candidates came together over a meal to pledge their commitment to winning the general election.

The news media swarmed the event like flies around . . . a spilled milkshake. Six or seven candidates sat at a long table at a neighborhood breakfast spot while the cameras whirred and clicked, capturing this anomalous camaraderie. Then, after about four minutes, the press left. One candidate subsequently left as well; once the cameras were gone, she had little interest in breakfast or unity. But the rest of us stayed, sitting there somewhat awkwardly as we waited for our pancakes and eggs.

Then something fascinating happened. The group had zero interest in talking about politics, or even current events; we'd had plenty of that. Instead, we all started talking about our childhoods. There was a striking consensus among this diverse group, all of whom had grown up in different places under different circumstances, that kids today were being deprived of what we had enjoyed most: just running out the door on any given day and having fun.

I have heard the same complaint over and over again since becoming a parent: kids' sports are becoming incredibly structured and ridiculously competitive. There are eight-year-olds with private hitting coaches, and nine-year-olds being told that they have no future in a sport if they are not playing in competitive leagues during the off-season.

Families say that they can't leave town during spring vacation because their children have practices or tournaments. An increasing number of teenagers are getting Tommy John surgery (named for Major

League pitcher Tommy John), which is a radical procedure to repair a ligament tear in the elbow by replacing it with a tendon harvested from somewhere else in the body. Teenagers are having the surgery more often because they are being urged to throw harder and more frequently, and to throw pitches that put a particular strain on young arms, such as curveballs and sliders. Ironically, Tommy John, the guy for whom the surgery is named, thinks this is all nuts. He told *NBC Nightly News*, "Just let the kids be kids."

I suspect some of this may feel familiar to you, since you have lived it. My reaction has been somewhat different. I put on my academic hat, and I asked, Why is this happening? Why are so many people doing something that makes them unhappy? I found a bizarre but compelling explanation: our eight-year-olds are locked in an "arms race" that has implications long after they are done playing Little League.

Here's how it works with a real arms race: A country enjoys a strategic advantage if it has more (or better) weapons than another country. The key insight is that only relative advantage matters. If the United

States has one nuclear weapon and Russia has none, then the United States has a crucial military edge.

But the Russians wouldn't stand for that; they would build more nukes, prompting the Americans to invest in defense technology to preserve their military advantage. Fast-forward ten hypothetical years and the United States might have fifty thousand warheads. When the Russians match that—as they will—the Americans would be forced to develop a missile defense system to once again restore their military superiority.

Here's the futility of the arms race: both countries would have been better off if they had just stuck with the situation in which the Americans had one nuke and the Russians had none. Instead, they both spend hundreds of billions of dollars to end up in exactly the same strategic place—money that could have been better spent by both countries on something else. It's like an animal on a hamster wheel—it does a lot of exhausting running just to end up in the same place.

So what does this have to do with Little League? I am convinced that young athletes (or, more accurately, their parents) are locked in an arms race—

they are doing a lot of exhausting running to end up in the same place. More important, I don't think it ends when kids take off their sports uniforms.

Competitive athletic success is a zero-sum game. If everyone in the world became twice as good at playing baseball, there would still be the same number of college scholarships and professional athletes. Albert Pujols would still be a baseball superstar, not you. He would just be twice as good as he is now.[*] And if the pitchers became twice as good too, the games would look pretty much like they do now. Athletic success is all relative, unlike many other life activities (such as socializing or getting an education or performing a public service) in which one person's gain does not come at someone else's expense. If we all learn twice as much, we will all be smarter and more productive, and ultimately wealthier, healthier, and better off in

---

[*] Ironically, Albert Pujols is protected from the arms race. The agreement between the Major League Baseball owners and the Major League Baseball Players Association stipulates that spring training cannot begin more than thirty-three days prior to the start of the season. Our six-year-olds have less institutional protection from overly intense competition than our World Series winners do!

other ways. (By the way, *grades* are not synonymous with *learning*; I'll get to that in a moment.)

First, back to Little League: If having private coaches teach seven-year-olds to throw curveballs makes kids and families happier than they were twenty years ago, terrific. If, having grown up in this era, you don't see a problem with any of this, then skip ahead. I will fully concede that I might just be overly nostalgic for my childhood games of pick-up street hockey. (We really did play in the street; we had to move the goals whenever cars came by.)

But if that extra practice, coaching, and money spent on equipment, camps, and lessons comes at the expense of other activities (such as family vacations, riding a bike for fun, playing other sports, or doing something really crazy like playing "kick the can" in the backyard for a few hours), then our kids' lives are worse for it. And, more important, the message to our eight-year-olds is that the key to life is running faster than the next guy, without thinking about why they are running or where they are trying to go.

I am always prone to excess cynicism; I see social problems where others often do not. So I ran this idea by a high school and college friend of mine who is one of the purest and most gifted athletes I know. In high school, Bill lettered in football, basketball, and baseball. He played baseball in college. Bill also has a son who is a gifted athlete, putting him in a good position to compare youth sports across generations.

Here is what Bill had to say: "The competition is absolutely sucking the joy out of sports. It's no longer fun; it's just what kids do."

Wow. That's coming from a guy who read *Sports Illustrated* in elementary school.

Here is all I am asking you to do: look around every once in a while and ask yourself; *Have I created a race out of something that ought to be a journey?*

A journey involves following a passion. You identify a worthwhile goal and then work relentlessly in that direction. There are often tremendous external rewards, but the direction and motivation come from within.

A race involves running faster than everyone else, regardless of where they happen to be going. This, too, involves a lot of hard work and the potential for large rewards—but not much introspection. In a race, success is defined by how you finish relative to others. If you flounder, even briefly, then someone will pass you by.

I see the Little League mentality bleeding into higher education, which is what I know best. I see it when students become more obsessed with grades than with learning, or when credentials mean more than the accomplishments they represent. Let me describe two recent incidents that left me vaguely troubled, for reasons that I could not quite put my finger on until recently.

The first involved a student who walked into my office after a midterm exam. She was despondent that she was going to get an A- in the class. You read that correctly; her midterm grade was an A-; not a B-, not a D. An A-. And when I describe her as despondent, I am not using the word lightly. I spent at least half an hour trying to assuage her anxiety, to no avail. Finally, I asked, "What is it that you want to do in life that you're not going to be able to do because you got an A- in this class instead of an A?" She didn't have an answer.

The second incident was a conversation with an

extremely successful entrepreneur who was reflecting on his experiences at one of the world's most highly selective business schools, which I will not name here.* He was describing the ethos of competition at the school, which at times seemed more important than the material being taught.

I asked him the following question: Did he think that most of his classmates would prefer to have this prestigious business school education without the credential, or the credential without the education? In other words, would those accepted to the MBA program prefer to 1) attend all of the classes, learn from their impressive classmates, and immerse themselves in one of the world's great universities—but no one would know they had done so; or 2) get the diploma, and therefore the credential from this esteemed institution, but none of the learning.

He said number two, with no hesitation at all.

Both of these incidents struck me as wrong, though for reasons that I could not articulate—until I read

---

* It's Harvard.

an obituary for Apple Computer founder Steve Jobs, at which point it all became crystal clear. As a young man, Steve Jobs, one of the most creative and transformational business leaders ever, dropped out of Reed College, but he continued to audit classes. *He got the education without the credential!* Jobs later said that one of the classes he audited on calligraphy helped to inspire the fonts supported by the Macintosh computer.

The "life as a race" mentality sends a powerful signal to kids that they can't take risks, because that may lead to a C, which will doom their chances of getting into a good college, or a good law school, or some other competitive endeavor. And then life will suck, just like not making the traveling soccer team.

Yet we know that success is not about simply running faster than everyone else in some predetermined direction. It is about finding a passion, taking risks, running in new directions, and dealing with failure.

If you think of life as a race, then every setback means that you have fallen behind. Every risk has a potential failure lurking nearby.

But if you think of life as a journey, then every

setback helps direct you to a place where you will be more likely to succeed. Every risk has a potential adventure behind it, or at least a learning experience. You are not necessarily in competition with everyone around you.

Is all of this really a problem? You tell me. This is the only section in the book whose title is followed by a question mark: Help stop the Little League arms race? Maybe it's a stretch to blame a broader social pathology on hypercompetitive soccer parents. Still, there is not a huge downside to asking every once in a while, Why am I doing this?

We will know for certain that my analysis is wrong when we see the following obituary: "Bob Smith died yesterday at the age of 74. He finished life in 186th place."

Read obituaries.

Obituaries are just like biographies, only shorter. They remind us that interesting, successful people rarely lead orderly, linear lives. I defy you to find a single obituary that begins, "Jane Doe won the Nobel Prize in large part because she was admitted to a prestigious, highly selective preschool. After that, everything just kind of fell into place." Instead, you will read about dead ends, lucky coincidences, quirky habits, excessive self-confidence (often interspersed with bursts of excessive self-doubt), and a lot of passion for something.

People who change the world often clash with the establishment first—because they see things differently. They drop out or get fired (or both in the case of Steve Jobs). And then, somehow, the world catches up. Every life story is different in an interesting way, which is the point. Some are inspiring. Some are tragic. Some are ironic. But every obituary I have read has helped me worry less about small setbacks; each one reminds me that life is just bigger than all that.

Of course, an obituary is also what people say about you when you are gone, literally. Phrases like "survived by seven ex-wives" and "challenging personality" and "estranged from his children" suggest that the person in question might not have thrived in building the kinds of human relationships I described earlier. Famous people are not always happy people— and vice versa. In any case, it's instructive to read an objective assessment of someone else's life.

The British news magazine *The Economist*, which has readers in roughly a hundred countries, runs one obituary in every issue. The point is not that just one globally important person dies a week, or even that the person selected is the most noteworthy person to have passed away in that stretch, but rather that the person selected led a particularly interesting and instructive life. It is often someone you have never heard of. Here are two recent examples, from issues picked nearly at random off of my coffee table:

Bill Smith, a Liverpool-born mountain and hill runner, aged 75: He didn't want level surfaces or follow-the-leader crowds. True adventure was to be alone. The terrain he traversed was steep slippy grass, or sheer clumps of rock where you had to climb or jump. Sometimes only shepherds or sheep had been that way before. Often you found your way just by eye and compass . . . His best day occurred on one of the several occasions when he did the Bob Graham Round— 42 Lakeland fells over 66 miles, with nearly 30,000 feet of ascent and descent, in less than 24 hours . . . On the flank of Skiddaw, looking up at the great grey mountain, he suddenly lost heart. But "Come on, lad," one of his pacers urged him. "You've nearly cracked it."

He ran for almost 40 years with a club, the Clayton-le-Moors Harriers, and spent much of that time giving the same encouragement to others. A runner gasping up to a summit cairn would get his cheery smile and his admonition to "Dig deep, lad." He would be seen stood in a puddle for an hour or more, holding a gate open for runners to pass. When he failed to turn up outside the Ram Inn to marshal the Thieveley Pike fell race on September 28th, it was the first hint that something was amiss.

Tiger Pataudi, Indian cricket star and national team captain, aged 70: His nickname, "Tiger", dated from childhood, but seemed to fit his style of play: whether his fierce competitiveness at bat, hooking and driving the ball to dig India out of some hole or another, or his elegant fielding in the covers, racing with easy grace to scoop and return, or his eager crouch in the gully, waiting to destroy . . .

Yet his true heroism sprang from handicap. He had one eye. The right one had been lost in a car accident in England in 1960, apparently eclipsing at its outset his cricketing career. But his ambition was undamaged. Within weeks, he was in the nets again, practicing, and within months he was playing Test cricket against the West Indies, against some of the fastest bowling in the world . . . He went on to score, over his career, 2,793 Test runs that included six centuries. No one knew how. He explained that in fact he saw two balls, and hit the inside one. With two good eyes, who knows what he might have done.

See what I mean?

Take time off.

When I say "time off," I don't mean Sunday afternoon or a long weekend. I mean reasonably long stretches of time that allow you to do things that would not otherwise be possible. Explore the world. Step away from your day-to-day existence and think more deeply about yourself. Or do both at the same time.

If you have just finished high school, think about taking a year off before college.

If you have just finished college, think about taking a year off before going to work.

If you are already at work, find a way to take some kind of retreat or sabbatical that allows you to recharge and reflect.

Remember, this book is about the things that I wish someone had told me as I was preparing to graduate from college. By the middle of my senior year, I had resolved to travel around the world during the year after college, and it was a very lonely decision. I wish I could tell you that my classmates were supportive of my decision. They were not. If anything, there was a somewhat hostile reaction from classmates who were in the throes of corporate recruiting, which in hindsight still disappoints me.

My traveling companion, Leah, who is now my wife, encountered a variation on the same basic reaction. Leah had interviewed for jobs before our trip. All of the firms she was interested in ran large training programs; each year a new crop of college grads would enter the program at the same time. She assumed that she could defer any of these programs for a year and begin work with the next "class" of recruits. She ended up getting a job with a prestigious consulting firm. That was step 1 of her grand plan.

But step 2 didn't work out as planned. The firm

told Leah quite emphatically that she had to start work with her "class" after graduation. If she wanted to travel for a year, fine. But she wouldn't have a job when she got back—unless she wanted to go through the whole interview process again the next year. No guarantee.

The decision was stark: take a very attractive job, or give it up and travel the world with her idealistic, unemployed boyfriend.

Leah decided to travel the world. On a campus temporarily obsessed with getting jobs, that was a puzzling and provocative thing to do. One remarkable incident encapsulates the reaction. A classmate and good friend walked up to Leah in a fraternity basement and said, "I heard you're being really stupid."

I wish I could tell you that my family was supportive. They were not. (For an explanation of parents in general, see Number 7½.) I love my parents dearly. They are broadly supportive. But they did not support this particular decision. I vividly remember sitting across the kitchen table from my mother, explaining my postgraduation plan to head west to

California and just keep going: Tahiti, New Zealand, Australia, Indonesia, China, India, Eastern Europe, Western Europe, London, New York.

My mother said, "But when you get back, you'll be a year behind."

"Behind what?" I replied.

Taking that year to travel was the single most formative experience in my life. Here is why:

Because it was like a fifth year of college (at less than half the price). In theory, we go to college to prepare for life. We learn to think more critically. We gain a greater appreciation for everything from history to the physical environment around us. We dabble across disciplines in hopes of finding a subject that grabs us. We get an education because it makes us more complete and capable human beings.

So does exploring the world. In college, I took a course called Monsoon Asia—which made a lot more sense when I found myself standing in an Indonesian rice paddy several years later. I took another class on global food and hunger; it was a great course, but still less impactful than spending ten minutes at the main train station in Calcutta.

Much of our postcollege journey took place in 1989. We stood in the lobby of a hotel in Lhasa, Tibet, and counted the number of Chinese tanks rolling by as part of a bloody crackdown on native Tibetans protesting against Chinese rule. (The same thing would happen a few months later—on a bigger scale and with more public notice—in Tiananmen Square.) We were in Eastern Europe when the border was opened between Hungary and Austria—the first crack in what would eventually be the collapse of the Berlin Wall.

In nine months of traveling, I read more, I saw more, and I thought more than I did during any single year of college.

Because it is cheaper and easier than you think. I will readily concede that taking time to travel seems like a luxury. Yet our entire trip cost roughly the same as a Honda Civic, which certainly is no great luxury for most college graduates. (True, this was not high-end travel; I did literally sleep with goats on at least one occasion.) If you get a Honda Civic for graduation, that's certainly nice, but it's not the kind of gift that makes people say, "Wow, you're really lucky!" I am plenty lucky in life—but it wasn't luck or family wealth that propelled me around the world.

I worked at a law firm for four months after graduation. Armed with my Ivy League degree, my sole job was putting fifty-thousand documents in chronological order. I lived at home and caddied on the weekends. When I had enough money saved to buy a Honda Civic, I bought a one-way plane ticket to Sydney instead (with stops in Tahiti and New Zealand along the way).

My traveling companion, Leah, started with less. She grew up in a single-parent family. Her father died of cancer at a young age, leaving her mother with four children, the oldest of whom was six. It was a wonderful childhood, but Leah's mother, a preschool teacher, was not exactly passing out cash for world travel, or even for college for that matter. Leah took out student loans to finance her education. After graduation, she went to waitress on Nantucket, living in a boarding house on the grounds of a country club, working banquets on the weekend, and babysitting at night. When she had her "Honda Civic cash" saved, she prepaid her student loans for the year (a complete bureaucratic nightmare by the way) and then bought her one-way ticket to Australia.

If you want to explore the world, you can make it happen. I didn't say it was easy; I just said it was easier than you think.

Because it allows for extraordinary moments of reflection. You may take a year to go around the world, or several months to hike the Appalachian Trail, or six weeks to visit presidential libraries, or even a week to camp in the woods (assuming that you have turned off your iPhone). No matter what you do, if you are able to untether yourself from day-to-day responsibilities, you can free your mind in a way you might not otherwise experience.

It is never easy to step off what feels like a rapidly moving escalator. But if Bill Gates could do it regularly while he was CEO of Microsoft, you probably can too. Gates was famous for going alone to a secluded cabin for an entire week. He would stock up the refrigerator with diet soda. An employee would bring him two simple meals a day. Gates would read papers and books, contemplate the future of technology, and send notes to Microsoft employees sharing thoughts on all of these things. In short, he would intellectually recharge and search for big ideas that were apt to be lost among the day-to-day minutiae of running a company.

Because, ironically, it is a great career move. Despite my mother's fear that I would return "a year behind," the reality is that traveling the world changed my career trajectory for the better. Not immediately, of course. Remember, I came back with no money and no job. A year and a half after college graduation, I was living with a seventy-year-old couple in New Hampshire. But traveling allowed me to migrate professionally toward one of my great life interests: writing. Before I headed around the world, I arranged with a small regional newspaper in New Hampshire and Vermont to be its "traveling correspondent." For this, I was paid the princely sum of fifty dollars per article. My job was to find some story every couple of weeks that would interest local readers. I would write a column longhand (as there was no Internet at the time), shoot a roll of black-and-white film to accompany the piece, and then mail both back to White River Junction, Vermont. By the time we were done traveling, I had published sixteen or seventeen stories. I had accumulated what they call in the journalism business "clips"—which would later persuade a U.S. governor that I had sufficient proficiency to be his speechwriter.

Do you remember Leah's job with the consulting firm? It turns out that she wasn't being so stupid after all. She was really just engaged in a big game of "chicken" that ultimately ended in her favor. Given that the consulting firm was keen on hiring her right after graduation, there was no rational reason why they wouldn't be happy to have her one year later. Once she bought the one-way ticket to Australia, the firm realized that she had called their bluff. The firm agreed to let her defer the job for a year, but, to save face, they scheduled one final "re-interview" with a partner just days before we left on the trip.

Leah put on a suit and turned up for the interview at the appointed time. It turns out that the partner hadn't gotten the memo advising him to be skeptical of this whole travel endeavor. Rather than giving her the cold shoulder, the first thing he said was, "I wish I'd done this. Where are you going?" The balance of the time was spent discussing the specifics of the itinerary.

Because you will have extraordinary experiences that broaden and deepen your understanding of people and places. Leah and I set out to travel the world because we knew it was an alluring, exciting, exotic place. Little did we anticipate that one of our most memorable experiences would unfold in California. We began our trip in San Francisco. (This is when we stayed with my friend John and his mother and urged John to take the job offer in Saipan.) However, our flight to the South Pacific left from Los Angeles, so we needed to get from San Francisco to Los Angeles as cheaply as possible. And we had about thirty-six hours to do it.

We began by hitchhiking, with only mixed success. We made it about a hundred miles in one full day, leaving us a couple hundred miles from Los Angeles with only about twelve hours until our flight left. The only feasible option at that point was to take a bus for the balance of the trip. To do that, however, we first had to get to the bus station. We put our thumbs out, hoping to get a ride for just a couple of miles so that Greyhound could take us the rest of the way.

An older man picked us up. He was relatively small, in both height and stature, and meticulously dressed. I remember that he was wearing a suit and tie and that he had very elegant salt-and-pepper gray hair. He spoke with a vague, unrecognizable European accent. We told him that we needed to get to the bus station. He asked where we were going. I repeated that we were going to the bus station. He said, "Yes, yes, but where are you going?"

I said, "Los Angeles."

He looked at his watch and said, "I can take you there." But first, he said, he would like to go to his house and change into more comfortable clothes.

Los Angeles was two hundred miles away. I looked at this guy, who was probably seventy years old, and I thought, There is just no reason to believe that he is anything other than a distinguished old gentleman looking to help out. (A great deal of research confirms that—for better or for worse—these first impressions tend to be correct.) Besides, if our hitchhiking adventure went awry, even Leah could take this guy down. I explicitly remember thinking that.

So we got in the car.

I am writing this book, so you don't have to be a detective to infer that we did not become the victims of a serial killer. Still, I feel compelled to point out that you probably shouldn't accept rides from strangers—and you certainly shouldn't go back to their homes. I am not telling you that what happened next was particularly smart. I am telling you that it was extraordinary.

Alex was the man's name. We went back to his house, where we sat in his living room while he went off to change his clothes. The only unusual thing about his home was that it was decorated with posters and pictures of every contemporary American president, without any regard for political party. John F. Kennedy was right there next to Ronald Reagan.

We got in the car and began driving south toward Los Angeles. The flight didn't leave until midnight, so the pace was leisurely. We stopped for lunch. We stopped for frozen yogurt. We stopped so that Alex could rest in the shade for a while. At one point I mentioned that I had never seen the Pacific Ocean, so we stopped at a beach so that I could look at the Pacific Ocean.

Eventually we got to the airport in Los Angeles. Alex dropped us off, wished us well in our travels, and then drove off. I remember standing at the curb and waving good-bye as he pulled away.

You are probably wondering the same thing that I was for much of this long drive: Why was this guy willing to drive two strangers half the length of California? After four hours in the car, curiosity got the best of me. I asked.

To appreciate Alex's answer, you need just a little more detail. I was twenty-two. I was thin and tan. I had just gotten a crew cut to make life easier while traveling. I was carrying on my back a large pack with all of my possessions.

Alex told us that when he saw me by the side of the road, I reminded him of the American soldiers who had liberated him from a concentration camp at the end of World War II. He felt he owed a debt to those men, and to the whole country that had opened its doors to him. He tried to repay that debt whenever and wherever he could.

That was the beginning of our trip.

Your parents don't want what is best for you.

They want what is good for you, which is not always the same thing.

Let me back up and explain. My parents are adoring, supportive people. I would have dedicated this book to them, except that I dedicated my last book to them. Yet during a crucial period, from college until my early thirties, they disagreed with nearly every important decision I made. As noted earlier, they did not think I should travel around the world. They did not think I should try to write for a living. And they discouraged me from pursuing a PhD.

As I reflect on my most important life endeavors, they would probably be 1) traveling around the world, 2) deciding to write for a living, and 3) getting a PhD.

Do you see the pattern?

For years, I tried to unravel the mystery of how such well-meaning people could be such a pain in the ass* when it came to important life decisions. Then, when I became a parent, I figured it out. No parent wants to watch a child flounder or fail. There is a natural instinct to protect children from risk and discomfort—and therefore to urge safe choices. If I revisit the important life decisions that my parents objected to—traveling, writing, and getting a PhD—each presented a nontrivial risk of failure, emotionally, financially, or both.

Theodore Roosevelt, soldier, explorer, and president, once remarked, "It is hard to fail, but it is worse never to have tried to succeed." I love that quote, but I am willing to bet that Teddy's mother wanted him to be a doctor or a lawyer.

I find this risk-reward tension to be particularly

---

* A technical term often used by academics to mean "difficult; prone to offering resistance."

salient for my students from immigrant families, whose parents have worked hard to achieve comfort and stability. Those parents want to protect what they have attained by educating their children to become engineers and doctors—professions that are respectable, lucrative, and safe just about anywhere in the world, during any period of time.

Of course, when the children of those parents become my undergraduate students, they often tell me that they would prefer to write plays or to open restaurants (endeavors that virtually ensure financial and emotional trauma). I empathize with the bold aspirations of those students—but also with the trepidation of their parents.

The Pulitzer Prize–winning writer Jhumpa Lahiri, whose parents immigrated from India, captured this inevitable tension in a wonderful autobiographical essay for *The New Yorker*. She wrote:

My father, who, at eighty, still works forty hours a week at the University of Rhode Island, has always sought security and stability in his job. His salary was never huge, but he supported a family that wanted for nothing. As a child, I did not know the exact meaning of "tenure," but when my father obtained it I sensed what it meant to him. I set out to do as he had done, and to pursue a career that would provide me with a similar stability and security. But at the last minute I stepped away, because I wanted to be a writer instead. Stepping away was what was essential, and what was also fraught. Even after I received the Pulitzer, my father reminded me that writing stories was not something to count on, and that I must always be prepared to earn my living in some other way. I listen to him, and at the same time I have learned not to listen, to wander to the edge of the precipice and to leap.

This lovely passage made me think three things: First, Jhumpa Lahiri's father would get along swimmingly with my mother. Second, I now more fully understand why Jhumpa has won the Pulitzer Prize and I haven't. Third, and most significant, this was the language I had been searching for. Most parents want some form of "tenure" for their children, even if it forecloses the option of a Pulitzer Prize. But if you, as a young graduate, want the Pulitzer Prize, you have to be prepared to go to the precipice and leap. You can't always expect your parents to be excited about that.

Don't model your life after a circus animal.

I suspect this was not something you were explicitly considering. Nor is this meant to pass judgment on the morality of making circus animals perform. I will leave that to someone else. My point here is that circus animals perform tricks because their trainers throw them peanuts or small fish for doing so. I am not an animal-training expert, but I am guessing that monkeys don't ride unicycles in skirts because they find it intrinsically rewarding, or because it was their life goal to ride a unicycle, or because they need the exercise. They ride unicycles because they want the peanuts. And if we gave them peanuts to do something else, like juggling while dancing to hip-hop, they would do that instead. As a new graduate, you should aspire to do better.

As you go through life, you will have all kinds of responsibilities and expectations. You will be a friend, a parent, a coach, a condo association president,* an employee, and so on. But only one of those responsibilities, your job, will typically earn you peanuts. By that I mean you will be explicitly evaluated and rewarded for your performance. You will get more peanuts for being particularly dedicated to your work. Over time, you may accumulate more peanuts than other people—and there is nothing inherently wrong with that. One of life's great rewards is finding work you love that also happens to be quite lucrative. (When you bought this book, I earned a fraction of a peanut.)

However, you will not get a review and peanuts for your performance as a parent. You will not get an impressive raise for carving out time to take your children to the zoo on a Wednesday afternoon. You

---

* This is one responsibility you should desperately try to avoid.

will get some feedback, of course. In my experience, teenage girls are generous in offering performance evaluations, which often involve words like "unfair," "mean," "ridiculous," and, as they spend more time prepping for the SAT, "charlatan." Then they demand help on their algebra homework.

You may get a formal performance evaluation of your marriage. That usually involves a judge and lawyers for each side. I am told it is extremely unpleasant and expensive—yet quite detailed in describing how you might have performed better as a spouse.

You will get periodic evaluations of your health and fitness from your physician. These doctors tend to use the same old shop-worn medical clichés like "lose 20 pounds" and "at risk of a heart attack" and "that is definitely *not* poison ivy." The good news is that if you don't go to the doctor regularly, you can avoid all of this hectoring. The bad news is that a heart attack can serve as its own impromptu and particularly harsh performance review.

I am not going to tell you what to do with your life. You may want kids; you may not. You may want to explore the world; you may not. You may consider it important to be civically engaged—or not. If you make a thoughtful appraisal of what is important to you in life, in these areas and many others, you are going to have a broad list. And, to circle back to where I began, nobody is going to give you short-term, explicit rewards for accomplishing any of the items on that list—except when it comes to work. In everything else, you won't have piles of peanuts with which to measure your success.

Not surprisingly, that brings me back to happiness research, which clearly reveals what provides us with a sense of satisfaction and well-being in the long run: healthy relationships with friends and family, exercise, hobbies, and purpose. The same research suggests that we tend to overestimate the satisfaction we will get from that next promotion and from the things we can buy with the extra salary, because we get used to them so quickly. We become habituated to a bigger house or a new car, meaning that after a short stretch, the extra square footage or the heated leather seats don't necessarily make us any happier than the old house or car did. The one exception is experiences, which, ironically, continue to make us feel happy long after they are over. Memories of our experiences are like pictures; we discard the bad ones and enlarge the good ones, making the latter seem more pleasing as time goes by. (I have noticed that my children always seem particularly well behaved in our vacation photos.)

The same research suggests one career-related activity that is likely to make you particularly *unhappy*: a long commute. This is not necessarily because the time spent in your luxury car is miserable (which is the part of the commute that most people think about), but because of the happiness-inducing activities that a long commute crowds out—exercise, socializing, hobbies, and so on.

In the same vein, I will offer you a different spin on what often gets described as "greed"—the relentless drive to accumulate wealth far beyond what anyone can rationally enjoy spending. My theory, and it is just a theory, is that we are all searching for meaning in our lives. We want to know "How am I doing?" or, near the end of life, "How did I do?" There is no overall life performance evaluation, with categories and points for all of the accomplishments that might matter. Was someone's life successful? We can't even define "successful," let alone quantify it.

We can, however, quantify whether someone has accumulated more peanuts than his or her peers. (Large houses, fast cars, and fancy handbags help to broadcast this fact.) The accumulation of wealth becomes an egregiously oversimplified yardstick for measuring life success.

Let me be explicit about what I am *not* saying here. I am not saying that you shouldn't work hard. If you think you will become exceptional at anything without lots of grinding away, you are delusional.

And I am *not* saying that there is anything wrong with getting rich. I teach economics. The wonder of a market economy is that you can only get rich by producing something that the rest of us want to pay for. And if we want to pay for it, that is usually because it's going to make our lives better. The private sector thrives by producing goods and services that people need and want: houses, food, medicine, entertainment, air fresheners, golf lessons, and so on.

I don't even have an inherent dislike of five-thousand-dollar handbags, if they make you five thousand times happier than a reusable grocery sack.

Here is my warning: there are a whole host of areas in your life that might be quite important to you but for which there will be no formal performance evaluation. Think about it this way: If you leave a work task undone in order to meet a friend for a pre-planned dinner, then you are "shirking" your work. True enough. But remember that shirking goes both ways. If you cancel dinner to finish your work, then you are shirking your friendship. That's just not usually how we think about it.

In other words, if you choose to ride a unicycle, or to juggle while dancing to hip-hop, do it because you have thought about how it will make your life better, not because someone is tossing you peanuts (or small fish) to do so.

Please note that I have used "peanuts" here as a metaphor; I realize that a puzzlingly large number of you have life-threatening peanut allergies. The content of this section notwithstanding, this book contains no nut products, nor did it come into contact with other books that may contain nuts.

It's all borrowed time.

I know that commencement is a happy time, but that does not preclude some deeper reflection. One of life's realities that becomes very clear after you leave college, and sometimes even before, is that you shouldn't take anything for granted—not this afternoon, not tomorrow, and certainly not twenty years from now.

You will recall that this book is based on my talk at Dartmouth's Class Day, an event that I had participated in twenty-three years earlier. One of our speakers that day was our class president, Karen Avenoso, who was also a good friend of mine. She was a Rhodes Scholar, a wonderful writer, a social activist, and an extremely kind and thoughtful human being. If I had to choose one person in our class who was most likely to go on to change the world in a positive and significant way, it would have been Karen—without even a second thought. In fact, I remember that her speech railed against the Dartmouth tradition of breaking clay pipes at the end of Class Day because it glorified tobacco use.

Karen died of a rare form of cancer before our tenth reunion. That happens in life. What it means for you, and what I have found to be one of the great challenges of adulthood, is that you must always balance present and future. If you aspire to great accomplishments in a decade or two, you need to grind away now. You need to do work that you would prefer not to do, to spend time on tasks that you don't particularly enjoy. Frankly, that is an important part of your twenties. Sorry to be the bearer of that message.

But you can't lose sight of the fact that there are no guarantees in life. If you grind away miserably to become a CEO, no one can promise you that it will work out that way, or that the sacrifice will be worth it even if it does.

On the other hand, if you spend most of your time skateboarding with friends and playing video games,

I can pretty much assure you that your professional accomplishments will be limited.

You have to navigate that trade-off. On this point, I do have advice, which is to take joy in the journey, rather than building your life around how good you expect the view to be when you get to the top. When Leah and I traveled around the world, we spent a short time at a hill station in West Bengal, India. We had only a day or two. The locals insisted that we take a hike to the top of a nearby mountain, which supposedly offered a stunning view of the Himalayas at sunrise. The hike was long—I want to say at least six miles each way—and we had to get to the top by sunrise, so that meant starting long before dawn.

We walked. And we walked. It wasn't a rigorous climb. Instead, the road and trail wound through lots of small villages. As we plodded along, mile after mile, what we saw was rural India waking up: farmers heading to their fields, shopkeepers taking deliveries, children doing chores before school—all of the prosaic details of human existence that turn out to be beautiful in their totality. Suffice it to say that when the sun finally rose, the day was foggy—so foggy that at the top of our climb, Leah and I had trouble seeing one another, let alone the Himalayas. We took one picture, just for the humor of it, and all we got was a shot of gray nothingness.

It was an awesome hike. We headed back down knowing that we were having one of the great days of our trip. And obviously, it was all about the journey and not the view at the top. To this day, that specific hike is the metaphor I keep in mind when taking on life projects that may or may not work out, like spending seven years writing a textbook or running for Congress in a field of twenty-three candidates. I try to ask myself, Is the journey still worthwhile if the mountain turns out to be enshrouded in fog at the top?

Academics like to formalize things, so I propose to you the "hit by a bus" rule. Here is the test: Would I regret doing this, spending my life this way, if I were to get hit by a bus next week, or next year?

Of course, there is an important corollary: What if I don't get hit by a bus? Does this path lead to a life that I will be pleased with and proud of in ten or twenty years?

There are plenty of endeavors that will comfortably pass both of those tests. One of my favorite freelance assignments was writing a piece on Paul Tsongas, who ran for president as a Democrat in 1992. Tsongas was the first declared candidate against George H. W. Bush, who had an approval rating over 90 percent at the time. Tsongas was smart, but he was not well known, not a good speaker, and not charismatic. To his credit, he was the first candidate to speak candidly about the budget deficit, which was a problem then, too, but not something people wanted to hear about.

I was traveling with Tsongas for the story, and at one point I asked, "Do you really think you can win?"

He said, "I don't have to. I just have to run a race that my grandchildren will be proud of." He did.

I have no idea what the future will bring.

S eriously, no clue.

I am not that old. And yet when I reflect on the changes that have taken place since my graduation in 1988, they are staggering.

As my fellow students and I listened to our own Class Day speeches, we did not even conceive of anything remotely like the Internet. Not even a glimmer of a thought. But it was less than a half decade away.

When I applied to college, Osama bin Laden was on our side, fighting the Soviets in Afghanistan.

I typed that college application on an electric typewriter. I wrote one of my essays on Korean Airlines Flight 007, a commercial flight that was shot down for inadvertently flying into Soviet airspace. As we sat on the ground outdoors in 1988, who knew that the Berlin Wall would soon come crumbling down and that the cold war, the phenomenon that shaped my childhood just as 9/11 has shaped yours, would end precipitously before our fifth reunion?

On the other hand, I was an Asian Studies major and I focused on the Middle East. The Palestinian intifada was going on during my senior year. Of course, I didn't say "first intifada" because it didn't dawn on me—or anyone else—that nothing would change fundamentally after that conflict. Instead, we would just start numbering them: the first intifada, the second intifada, perhaps the third.

On the other hand, I suspect that most of us thought we would have beaten cancer and AIDS by now, as we did polio and smallpox. Not yet.

The Boston Red Sox did finally win a World Series. My Chicago Cubs still have not.

Some things change so fast and so significantly that it's hard, or at least amusing, to imagine what life was like before. Other things have not changed much at all, dispiritingly so in some cases.

When I first began to teach undergraduates, I was

invited to a barbecue at a fraternity. After the ice was broken, one of the guys came up and asked a curious question. He asked, "When you were a student and you had a party, how did you let people know?" After all, there was no Internet, no cell phones, no texting. So I told him. We printed up fliers, made copies, and hung them around campus. We wrote notes on the white boards that every student had on his or her dorm-room door.

This guy looked at me and said, "Wow, that is so cool."

Now fast-forward twenty years. We live in a world in which U.S. Representative Anthony Weiner can use his Twitter account to send photos of his crotch to thousands of people in a split second! Not so cool.

On a more serious note, as someone who has spent his adult life working in public policy, I think a lot about the contradictions, about how some things get better and better, while others don't change at all.

We put a man on the moon when I was two years old. Now I am forty-five, and hundreds of millions of people around the world still don't have access to clean water.

At the end of the day, it is all about the choices we make. Technology and globalization and the other forces of change are like a stream running downhill. We cannot stop them; we cannot turn them around. But we can direct them. We design the incentives, build the social institutions, mediate the disputes, make the laws, and decide how our collective resources will be used or not used, shared or not shared. We, as educated and responsible adults, have the ability to shape and direct the inexorable forces as they come spilling downhill.

Change is inevitable; but progress depends on what we do with that change.

And that brings us to commencement. When my class was sitting at Class Day in 1988, nobody said to us, "Hey, we've given you a bunch of courses on the Internet so that you'll be ready when it appears in five years." There was no class on what we should do on September 12, 2001. Instead, like you, we studied history, and economics, and languages, and philosophy, and constitutional law, and religion.

We graduated, as will you, perfectly equipped to deal with nothing! And yet we left well equipped to deal with everything.

Don't try to be great.

This may seem like a counterintuitive ending. I have just finished giving you life advice. You are a new graduate, and the world lies before you. You are supposed to head out into the world determined that you can invent things, improve lives, make money, and so on. I hope, despite the fact that my advice to this point has been rooted more in reality than in cheerleading, that you will still feel that way.

But this last tidbit comes from a journalist in Chicago, Phil Ponce. Phil is the host of a news program on public television called *Chicago Tonight*. The point of the program is to discuss serious issues in the news, not to get guests arguing and yelling at one another. (Weird, right?) One of Phil's jobs is to elevate the performance of his guests—to make them as interesting and informative as they can be during the half hour or so that they are on his program.

The show is filmed live, meaning that if you blunder incoherently or fall off your stool, hundreds of thousands of people will immediately see it. I was once a guest on Phil's show, and as I sat on the set with the other guests, just thirty seconds from airtime, this was pretty much what was going through my head: Would I be witty and convincing? Would the other guests look more knowledgeable and impressive? How should I balance on my seat so as to look comfortable without toppling over during the program?

And it was at that moment that Phil leaned over to all of us and said, "Don't try to be great. Just be solid." Then the cameras went on.

That simple advice had a profound effect. *Because I knew I could be solid.* That was within my control. I could just talk about what I knew. I could answer questions candidly. I could have a fun and interesting conversation with the other guests. I might have some funny quips; I might not. Phil's advice was liberating because it removed the pressure to deliver what I wasn't certain I could deliver. And it made me better at doing what I knew I could.

I think about Phil's admonition when I sit down to write the draft of a chapter for a new book. If I believe that those first few sentences have to be beautiful prose, then it's going to be a long, unpleasant day. Instead, if I just focus on getting a subject and verb into every sentence, then I can write comfortably. Sometimes beautiful prose happens; if not, that's what future drafts are for.

If you are a golfer, trying to be great will make you tighten up. And if you get "tight," then you are apt to leave a six-foot putt about five feet short (based on my experience).

If you are a businessperson, trying to be great will make you too risk averse. And if you are too risk averse, you will miss the very opportunities that launch great business careers.

If you are a politician or community leader, trying to be great will make you too resistant to compromise, which is often exactly what the circumstances require. If I were advising a newly elected president, I would absolutely tell him or her to aspire to be solid rather than great.

Being great involves luck, and unique circumstances, and lots of other forces beyond your control. You can't just make it happen by working more or trying harder.

There is an irony here, of course. The less you think about being great, the more likely it is to happen. And if it doesn't, there is absolutely nothing wrong with being solid.

Good luck and congratulations.

Acknowledgments

This all began with the Dartmouth Class of 2011. Thank you. I remain deeply grateful for the honor and privilege of speaking at your Class Day. I would particularly like to thank Joseph Coleman, president of the Class of 2011, for extending the invitation.

This book obviously started as a speech. Only when the transcript of the speech began bouncing around the Internet did it dawn on me that the themes I touched on had struck a chord. As usual, my agent Tina Bennett immediately saw the potential of the project and ushered it along. As she read the manuscript, we realized that our lives had more points of intersection than we'd ever imagined, including the joy of knowing my Dartmouth classmate Karen Avenoso and the sorrow of losing her so young.

Drake McFeely at W. W. Norton offered the vision

and guidance necessary to transform a relatively short speech into a more substantive piece of work. If Drake was the architect, then Jeff Shreve was the guy at Norton wearing the hard hat every day so that the project actually got done. I find it a joy to work with people who take such pride in producing great books.

Peter Steiner's illustrations brought a smart and funny sensibility to the book. I cannot draw. I have no training in the visual arts (other than regularly reading cartoons in *The New Yorker*). So it was a complete delight to send text off to Peter and get his fresh and clever drawings back a few days later. Peter is a fabulous partner, and his unique talent has enriched this project.

My research assistant Katie Wade can track down the most obscure facts and figures. It was Katie who not only found the photo of the tobacco executives testifying before Congress but also documented all their Ivy League degrees.

My parents became anxious as soon as word leaked out that they were mentioned in the book. (I'm now fairly certain that my oldest daughter was responsible for that leak.) They needn't have worried, as I trust the text makes clear. I hope that I can always provide my children with such love and steadfast support. Of course, I also hope that my children will ignore some of my well-intentioned advice *on occasion*, as I did with my parents.

Many parts of this book are an homage to my wife Leah. She was with me at our own Class Day in 1988, and she has been with me ever since. (For the record, she does not really wear her Phi Beta Kappa ribbon around the house.) I do believe that life is a journey, and on that journey I have been blessed with an extraordinary companion.

Notes

21 "That the only thing that really matters": Quoted in Joshua Wolf Shenk, "What Makes Us Happy?" *Atlantic*, June 2009.

21 "The overall impression": David Brooks, "The Sandra Bullock Trade," *New York Times*, March 29, 2010.

49 "ability to cope with frustration": Yuichi Shoda, Walter Mischel, and Philip K. Peake, "Predicting Adolescent Cognitive and Self-Regulatory Competencies from Preschool Delay of Gratification: Identifying Diagnostic Conditions," *Developmental Psychology*, vol. 26, no. 6, 1990.

50 "life is a parade": David Brooks, "Marshmallows and Public Policy," *New York Times*, May 7, 2006.

52 "To be able to delay immediate satisfaction": Yuichi Shoda, Walter Mischel, and Philip K. Peake, "Predicting Adolescent Cognitive and Self-Regulatory

Competencies from Preschool Delay of Gratification: Identifying Diagnostic Conditions," *Developmental Psychology*, vol. 26, no. 6, 1990.

57   "Just let the kids be kids": Tommy John, *NBC Nightly News*, June 6, 2005.

64   obituary for Apple Computer founder Steve Jobs: "A Genius Departs," *Economist*, October 8, 2011.

69   "Bill Smith, a Liverpool-born": "Bill Smith," *Economist*, October 22, 2011.

70   "Tiger Pataudi, Indian cricket star": "The King of Indian Cricket," *Economist*, October 1, 2011.

90   "It is hard to fail": "Theodore Roosevelt Quotes," American Museum of Natural History, http://www.amnh.org/common/faq/quotes.html.

91   "My father, who, at eighty": Jhumpa Lahiri, "Trading Stories," *The New Yorker*, June 13, 20, 2011.